"Learning and Growing Together"

Author: Ebony S. Cuffee
"This book is dedicated to The Empowered Lounge Foundation."

A Message from Mrs. Cuffee:
Dear Teachers,

As we step into each new day, we hold an incredible opportunity to ignite curiosity and excitement in our students. It's easy to fall into the routine of lessons, but let's never forget the power we have to shape their love for learning. When we bring energy, enthusiasm, and passion into our classrooms, we offer our students more than just knowledge – we give them a reason to be excited about school.

I urge you to keep inspiring. Show your students that learning isn't just important – it's fun, rewarding, and filled with endless possibilities. Together, we can rekindle their excitement for education, one lesson at a time.

Let's strive to be the teachers who not only educate but also light up our classrooms with joy, wonder, and the belief that every student can grow, thrive, and achieve their dreams.

With gratitude and excitement,
Mrs. Cuffee

"Good morning, class!" Mrs. Cuffee said excitedly, greeting the students with a big smile.

"Good morning, Mrs. Cuffee," the class responded, but their voices were grumpy and sleepy.

"It's learning time, so all of you need to wake up! Learning is so much fun!" Mrs. Cuffee cheered as her energy filled the room.

"Learning is fun, but it's too early, and I want to go back to bed," Kingston said sadly, his head dropping onto his desk with a soft thud.

Mrs. Cuffee walked over to Kingston's desk and gently patted him on the back. "Kingston, we come to school to learn and grow. If we're not learning, then we can't... what, class?" she asked with a twinkle in her eye.

"We can't grow!" the class replied in unison, their voices raised with excitement as they remembered the important lesson Mrs. Cuffee always taught them.

"Mrs. Cuffee! Mrs. Cuffee!" Kenya yelled loudly, raising her hand while jumping out of her seat. Mrs. Cuffee took a deep breath, trying to stay patient. "Yes, Kenya?"

"Can I go to the nurse? I think all of this learning is making me feel nauseous!" Kenya said, looking a little green.

Mrs. Cuffee's smile faded, and she sighed. "What is going on with everyone today?" she asked, feeling frustrated.

"Why do we have to learn every day?" Kingston suddenly asked, slumping in his chair.

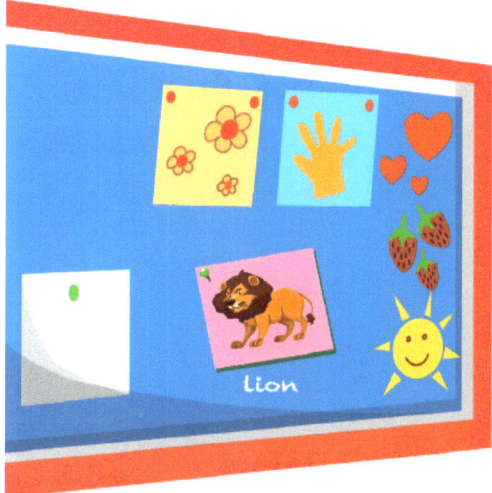

"Learning is fun, especially when you really like something," Mrs. Cuffee responded, her eyes lighting up. "Like science!" she exclaimed, jumping with joy.

"Science is pretty cool!" Hezekiah chimed in, his face brightening. "My dad takes my sister and I to the science aquarium all the time. We have so much fun looking at the cool sharks and snakes!"

Mrs. Cuffee rubbed her hands together, excited. "Exactly! Science is fun because we get to observe and experiment with the world all around us. And you know what? Science includes learning about sea animals, too!"

"Did you know an octopus is a sea animal that has three hearts, nine brains, and blue blood?" Mrs. Cuffee asked as the class stared at her eyes twinkling.

"Wow, really?" Kenya asked, wide-eyed.

"That's right!" exclaimed Mrs. Cuffee with excitement. "Octopuses have three hearts: two pump blood through the gills to absorb oxygen, while the central heart circulates the oxygenated blood to the rest of the body, providing energy to the octopus's organs and muscles."

"No way!" Kingston said, shaking his head in disbelief as the class started chatting excitedly, amazed by the octopus fact.

"Wow, octopuses are amazing!" Kingston exclaimed. "Mrs. Cuffee, can we go on a field trip there soon? We'd be so excited to come to school every day, especially on the day of the trip!"

"Kingston, you are hilarious," Mrs. Cuffee replied, glancing at him out of the corner of her eye, trying not to laugh.

"Now, class!" Mrs. Cuffee said, raising her voice with excitement. "Raise your hand if you knew that octopuses have three hearts, nine brains, and blue blood."

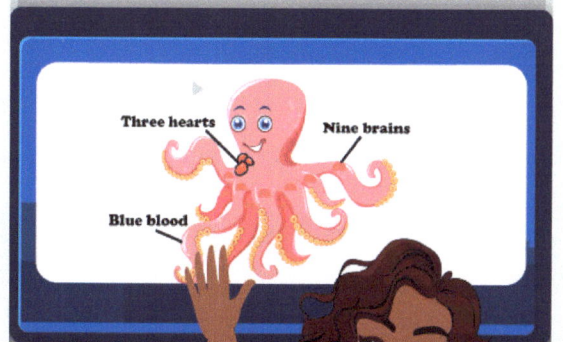

The class looked around at each other, and not a single hand went up.

"See, class?" Mrs. Cuffee said with a grin. "Learning is fun! And as you grow older, you'll keep discovering amazing things every day!"

Learning is fun

"What else can we learn about that's fun?" Kingston asked, his eyes wide with curiosity.

"I'm so glad you asked and seem ready to learn!" Mrs. Cuffee said, her face lighting up with excitement. "When you come to school, you grow and discover new things!"

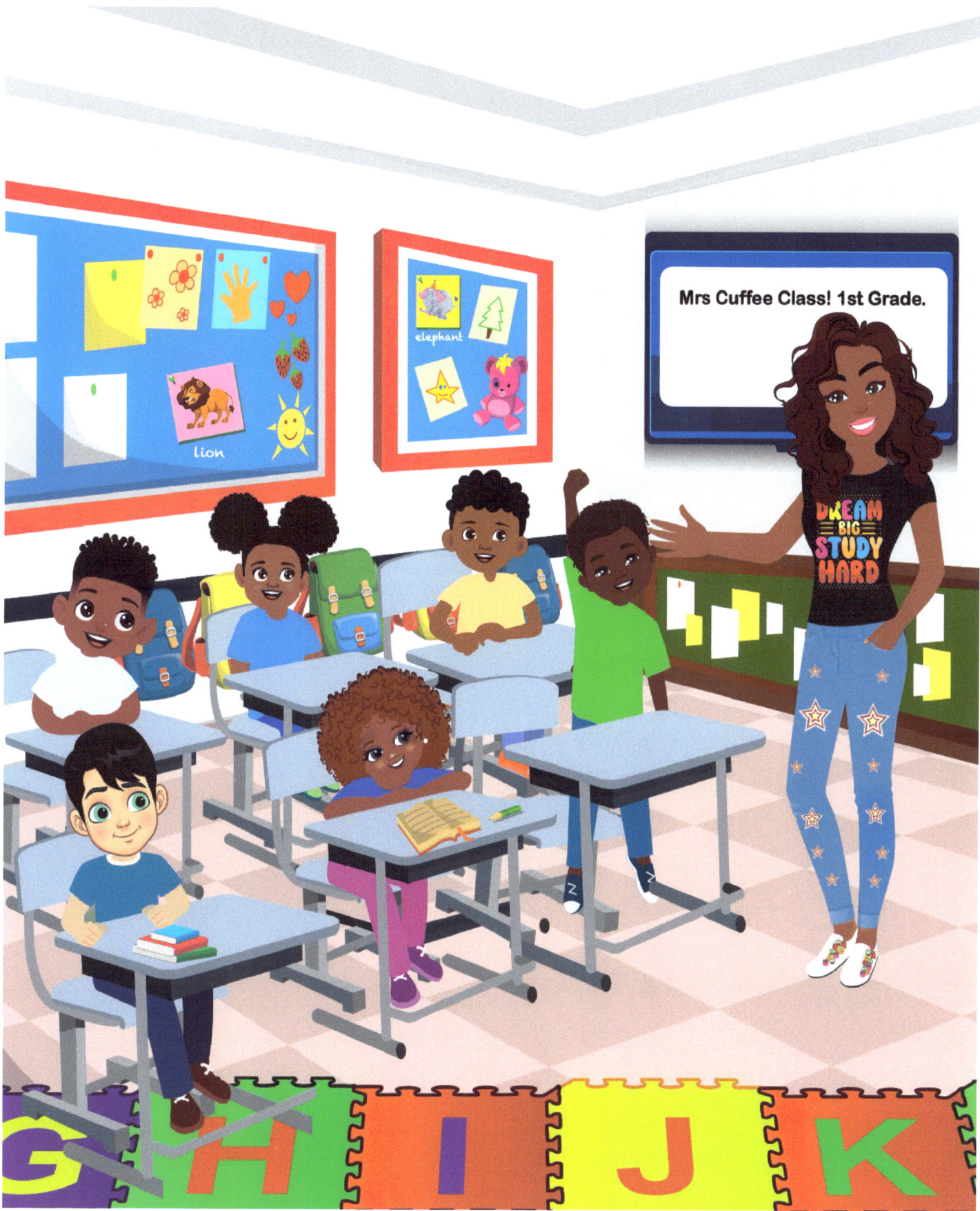

Mrs. Cuffee continued, "For example, you'll remember how to solve math problems like… 2 + 2 equals what, class?"

"Four!" the class yelled happily, all eager to answer.

"That's it!" Mrs. Cuffee exclaimed, bouncing with joy. "You're starting to get the groove of growing because you're learning!"

And soon, you'll also remember where we live. What country do we live in?"

"The United States!" Kingston shouted proudly. Kyle gave Kingston a high-five for getting it right, and Kingston blushed, smiling.

"That's right, Kingston! Now that's history!" Mrs. Cuffee cheered.

"L-E-A-R-N spells what, class?" Mrs. Cuffee asked with a grin.
"It spells the word 'learn'!" the class shouted together.

"Exactly!" Mrs. Cuffee clapped with joy. "Now you're all reading and writing! How excellent!"

The students smiled, beginning to understand why learning was so important.

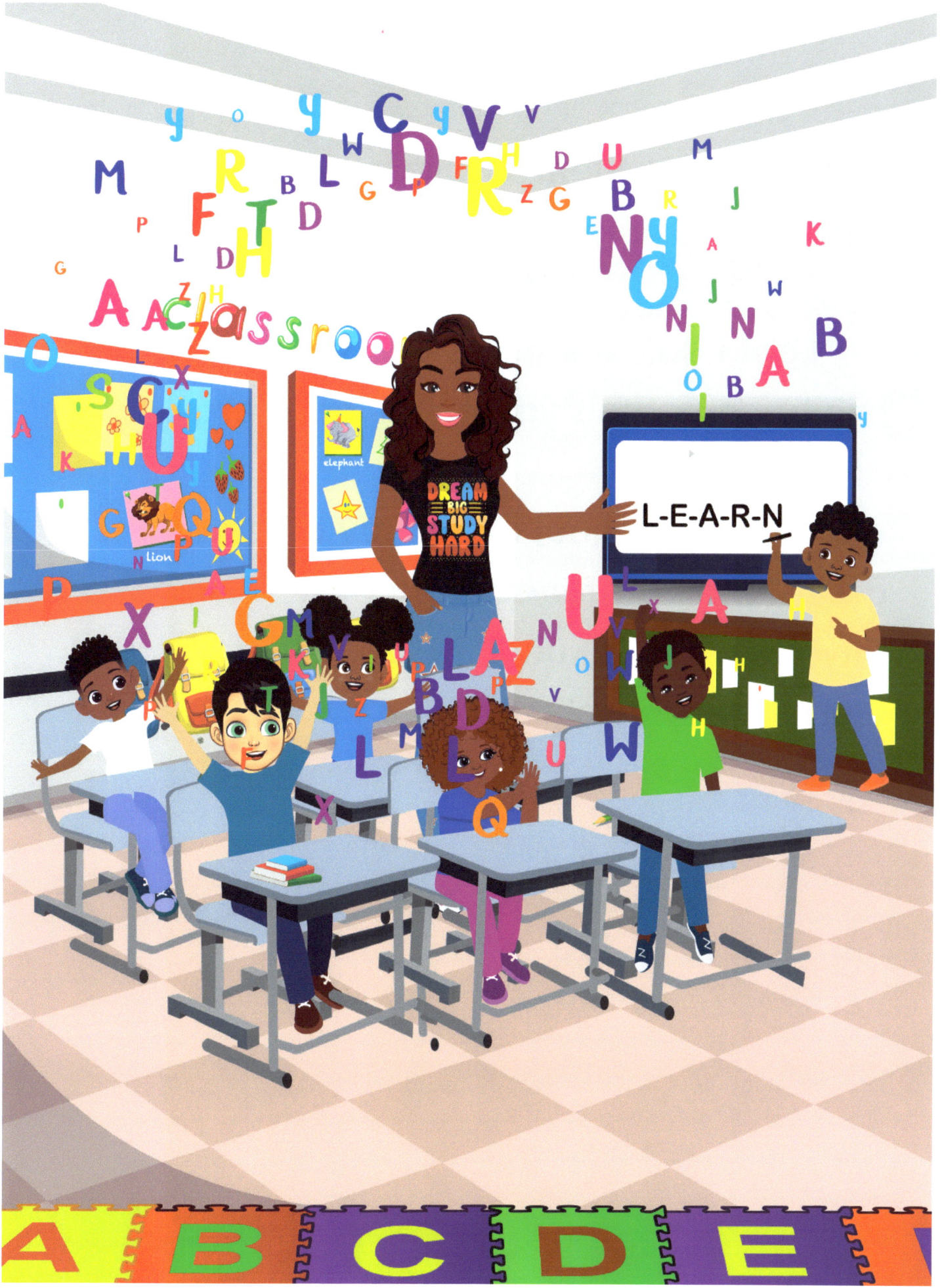

"Who thinks learning is more fun now?" Mrs. Cuffee asked.

"I do! I do!" the class shouted with excitement, their voices full of energy.

"We come to school every day to learn and grow," Mrs. Cuffee said proudly. "Does anyone want to know the best part about learning in this class?"

The students looked at each other, curiosity lighting up their faces.

"Me!" Mrs. Cuffee exclaimed, her eyes sparkling with enthusiasm. "I'm the best part because I love it when all of you grow and learn with me!"

www.ingramcontent.com/pod-product-compliance
Lightning Source LLC
Chambersburg PA
CBHW042020080426

42735CB00002B/115